My Late Mother
as a
Ruffed Grouse

Will Nixon

6-7-08

Frank,
Thanks for being here
today for the reading.
Enjoy!
Will

FootHills Publishing

Acknowledgments

Many of these poems first appeared, sometimes in different versions, in the following publications: *Art:Mag, Ashes, Ashes, Barbaric Yawp, Bellowing Ark, Bryant Literary Review, The Cafe Review, California Quarterly, The Cape Rock, Chiron Review, Chronogram, Coal City Review, Confrontation, The Country and Abroad, Elysian Fields Quarterly, Friction, Hedge Apple, Hawai'i Pacific Review, Hunger, Into the Teeth of the Wind, The Ledge, The Literary Gazette, Main Street Rag, Metroland, Monocacy Valley Review, Oyez Review, Pearl, Phoebe, Pilgrimage, The Powhatan Review, Prima Materia, Rattle, The RBS Gazette, Salvage, Slipstream, Turtulia Magazine, Wisconsin Review.*

"When I Had It Made" and "Dead Wasps, Black Trees, Sugar Stars" appeared in the chapbook *When I Had It Made.*

"Dyslexic," "Blood Brothers," "Easy Out," "The Philosophy of Margaritas," and "Insomnia" appeared in the chapbook *The Fish Are Laughing.*

"Blood Brothers" and "The Philosophy of Margaritas" appeared in *The Second Word Thursdays Anthology.*

"My Late Mother as a Ruffed Grouse" appeared in *Vanguard Voices of the Hudson Valley.*

"Sister Scarecrows" and "The Life of the Stag" appeared in *Riverine: An Anthology of Hudson Valley Writers.*

Cover art by Carol Zaloom

ISBN: 978-0-941053-72-3

FootHills Publishing
P. O. Box 68
Kanona, NY 14856
www.foothillspublishing.com

For Saul,
who nurtured these poems.

For Emma,
who nurtured many of these years.

Contents

When I Had It Made

I had loose teeth that became nickels
under my pillow, a wooden trunk filled
with plastic pirate gear, and a black eye patch
my mother wouldn't let me wear
to second grade. I trapped crickets
in jelly jars and fed them grass blades,
until they died and joined
my collection of dried star fish, rocket stamps,
and Canadian pennies. I practiced lassoing
with the laundry line and almost caught
the squirrel my mother hated for running
in the roof gutters whenever
she tried to nap. One day I crawled
out from my window and climbed
the sandpapery roof shingles
to the crest of the house,
where I sat practicing for an unsaddled horse,
and saw things I'd never seen before:
the daisy window for the neighbor's attic
filled with lamps; the green hills
hunched like ants along the horizon,
where I bet some Indians still lived.
When the paper boy came, he didn't see me spying
and didn't know a black lab was racing
around the corner after his pants.
When Dad walked home, whistling
and swinging his briefcase, he didn't see me
almost as high as the crows.
He carried his gin-and-tonic onto the patio,
opened the newspaper to the Little League scores,
and told my mother in the kitchen
the next library lecture was about robins.
When I grew up, I decided, I would be an angel
who watched people like this all day.
I saw the first star at the end of the blue sky
and didn't come down,
until the sunset
put the smallest clouds to sleep.

Defending the Fort

In the dryer my wet sneakers thump like dinosaur heartbeats.
My model glue dries in my Messerschmidt.
Upstairs, my mother's feet walk on kitchen linoleum
that sounds like tape coming unstuck, needing to be fixed.
"Add it to the list," said my father before leaving:
the list I never saw, though I had to be on it for my slip
carving a pine wood derby car with an X-acto knife.
The scar above my knee looks like a purple worm.

I turn up the television for *The Wild Wild West*,
so my mother won't hear me walk on the padded pipe,
leading like a balance beam from the washing machine
around the corner, squeezed between the panel board wall
and cold cement, to the window like a bunker hatch.
I shinny up into the crawl space of dry dirt
and dim light under my mother's bedroom,
a place so secret not even the snakes leave tracks.

I'm plotting victory for G.I. Joe in desert camouflage,
striding his Sherman Tank with rolling treads.
Killed fifty times already without a broken part,
he's not afraid of Hitler, Ho Chi Minh, or Michael Chippetta,
who fixed his plastic flintlock to fire acorns last autumn.
Now the retired dentist in the yellow house between us
has gotten so mad about weeding oak saplings
he's threatened my mother he'll get a Doberman pinscher.

Acorns forbidden, I've gathered chestnuts, walnuts, butternuts,
and peach pits for ammunition in G.I. Joe's sandy crater.
Every day he does a hundred push-ups, wipes dust
off the cannon, sits guard so squirrels won't steal
our ammo. He's read all my comic books.
He knows the next assault could be World War III.
It's my mother who doesn't understand the threat
of chocolate chip cookies smelling in the oven.
She'll ask where I got the dirt on my knees.

Dyslexic

The year I learned the hangman's noose,
I tied it everywhere: tire swings, clothes lines,
the drawstrings on the rec room curtains
that hung my pinkie purple during commercials.
"The doctor says you only want attention
because of your little brother," Mom said,
cupping her dishpan hands like horse blinders,
so she wouldn't see my purple finger, my eyelids folded
inside out like plum skins. My doctor didn't wear
a white coat, didn't depress my tongue
with an extra-wide popsicle stick. In a bow tie
always tilted to the side like a stopped propeller,
he played checkers and asked me easy questions,
like why I felt it necessary to pour dirt
down my brother's underwear. "Because I like to,"
I said; "besides, he doesn't care." My doctor never
smiled or frowned when I jumped his pieces,
sometimes three in a row. "Do you enjoy pulling
his pants down in public?" he asked.
"He doesn't care. He's dyslexic. Ask my mom."
"And what does dyslexic mean?"
"It means," I said, "he throws a baseball like a girl.
He gets to stay home from school in his bathrobe
because he didn't do his homework. He's fat,
and he'll eat ants if I tell him to."
My doctor suddenly jumped four pieces and chose red
for the next game. "I think it means you should be nice
to him," my doctor said. "Yeah," I said,
"but you're not his brother."

Mad Chemist

In the basement I fought World War One in dirt trenches
spread by trowel on the pool table. My metal soldiers
survived firecrackers catapulted by spoons, dive-bomb
hand attacks by my little brother, earthquakes from our knees
drumming under the table. My father stopped the war
when Rex the cat began pooping in the dirt: "Your mother
doesn't want you playing in bacteria."

So I played mad chemist. I'd invent acid for burning
open safes; freezing fluids for ants, worms, and girls' toes.
From brown bottles racked in my chemistry set, I mixed
bad odors and slow fizzles, but nothing burned from matches
dropped down blackened tubes. After my brother ratted,
my father locked the set in his closet: "Your mother
wants you to become a doctor, not a bomb maker.
Think about eating breakfast with no fingers."

I picked his closet with a paper clip and took my chemistry set
to the swamp with a bottle of Mountain Dew to mix my brother
a surprise. This formula would turn his hair blue, soften his teeth
like rubber. I drank my half of the Mountain Dew, then his half,
and held the bottle under slimy water, making it gurgle, until
a mucky head rose, a snapping turtle hooked like a claw.

My brother found the chemistry set in the swamp snow
rusty as an old can with spilled bottles of smelly ice.
My father punished me with no television for polluting
a wetland. He didn't know the secret of the snapping turtle:
sipping chemicals, glowing green, breathing fire.

My Secret Friend

Inside my grandfather's wooden radio
stood a model city of tomorrow
with glass tube towers of spiraling wires
and glass tube tunnels that could be highways on Mars.
But my father called it junk,
this set he'd heard *The Shadow* on,
stained with coffee rings on the walnut top
and stained with something yellow on the speaker cloth.

If I hadn't seen a radio just like it
on last night's *Untouchables*, my father said,
I never would have seen it now with all the other junk,
as we chased a raccoon out of the garage.
"Whatever you do," he warned,
after checking the kinked and dusty cord
with old masking tape as brittle as dried leaves,
"don't plug this in. It hasn't worked
since Truman, I'll bet. Remember, Truman
before Eisenhower. Eisenhower before . . .?"
My father wanted me to learn my presidents.

Only after convincing him
I needed a box to put my mouse cage on,
did he let me carry the radio up to my room.
That night after he wished me sweet dreams,
I turned the dial to cities I'd never seen:

"You got it! The master of the platters
from Detroit Motor City, number one home
of groove, stomp, and shout! Oh yeah,
we got the beat, the blues, the stereophonic
wrap-your-head-around-it all time
biggest good time your booty ever had.
Stay with it brothers, sisters, friendly visitors
from other planets. We're coming right back-at-ya
with the Shirelles on top of the hour."

By morning I could talk like that but saved it
for homeroom graham crackers and milk.
All the girls snickered
and said I was stuh-stuttering,
but Miss Beverly put down her chalk
and said, "Dig it, Daddy-o,
now how 'bout some 'rithmetic?"

My First Lesson in Electricity

In third grade I stripped two red wires,
coiled the copper ends round a flashlight bulb,
then plugged both wires into the socket beneath
the chalk tray. Like Ben Franklin I conducted
my own experiment in electricity. Instantly,
the bulb popped: smoking glass, blistered gray.
Miss Beverly, angry and resplendent
in her white calf boots, stood me up by the ear,
demanded to know why I wasn't dead.

I explained why I'd lived so long:
I ate my broccoli by holding my nose
and pretending it was pistachio ice cream.
I wore orthopedic shoes and didn't sit on public toilet seats.
I brushed my teeth counting to one hundred and one,
and cleaned the cedar shavings in my mouse cage
every Saturday, so my pet wouldn't spread germs.
It was Michael Chippetta who caught German measles
after fishing a foul ball from the sewer and using it again,
Tony Putrino who broke both legs sliding off his roof
with cigarettes. No; I swallowed my medicine
without making faces and still had my tonsils in.
I wasn't dead because I planned to live to one hundred and two
in a glass house on Mars with a butler kangaroo.

"Class," said Miss Beverly, steering me by the ear.
"We have a new lesson in what not to do."
She smelled like oranges in her orange miniskirt.
She had a stocking tear only I could see.
The boys seated with mimeographed sheets
stared at me with gray bulbs burning in their eyes,
which I learned that morning was jealousy.

My First Rubber

I bought my first rubber at Dirty Ed's fountain shop:
the grill was engine black, the hot dogs tasted like charcoal.
No one would eat a hamburger because we knew
Ed squeezed meatballs flat with his armpits.

We stole cop sunglasses from the counter carousel,
tipped Ed a nickel each. One of us hitchhiked,
five hid in the bushes. The woman who stopped
couldn't stop laughing. "You kids are so little league."
We worshiped her blonde hair flagging the open window.

We kicked sand castles, dove into water made silver
by our silver shades. We dodged bobbing jellyfish,
dressed the jerk who wasn't looking in a wig of seaweed
slimy as uncooked bacon. My rubber packet itched
inside my underwear. Someone shouted, "Don't fuck the fish."

The hot dog counter girls worked in bikinis dirty with grease.
I chose my first girlfriend, the blonde with sun freckles
between her breasts, and fingernails red as convertibles.
She looked up from her french fry vat. "What do you want?"
"You, baby." "Right, crater face." She made the fry baskets
crackle and spit. Her girlfriends giggled. We threatened
a mustard fight, then ran to break waves with our bony chests.

Heat Wave

The summer he stole a Zippo from Dirty Ed's fountain shop,
Chuckie Boyle torched anything you dared him to:
furry caterpillars flickered blue,
bug-spray cans roared like dragons,
model airplanes dripped flaming snot.
All he flubbed was farts. They refused to burn
like rocket engines the way Carl Jenkins saw in Scouts.

When Chuckie found his dad's coin collection unlocked,
he invited everyone to join us at the railroad tracks.
But Todd Smith was busy proving he could be
a Marine by swimming through jellyfish
then bragging it tickled. He wouldn't let us count,
but we knew he had thirteen welts on his back,
plus a dick like a radish.

Jed Patrick would have come, but he was fishing
for turtles in sewers. Brian Peters was grounded
for mooning Mrs. Hector's window. Charley Kahn
hadn't fixed his flat tire from a tack. Tim Barnes
slingshot squirrels for nickels at his aunt's bird feeder.
Jerry Simmons swallowed worms to gross out Billy Squire,
who'd puked after pulling a crinkled hair from his relish,
proof the retarded cook at the beach snack stand
flattened patties in his armpit before grilling burgers.
Richie Preston called his black cat Nigger.
The day a cop came to his house and stayed twenty minutes,
Richie wouldn't say what happened, but his dad
put up a brand new basketball net. Chuckie torched it.

Mikey Major hung out at the station but refused to help.
With a magic marker he made poster faces cross-eyed.
He said the ice cubes in a scotch glass ad secretly
spelled "SEX," but wouldn't show us how.
Who liked Mikey Major, anyway?
Mr. Moon Face Zits with jockstrap breath.
Chuckie and I laid the coins on the track ourselves,
a row of metal buttons to be flattened jackknife thin.

That night Mr. Boyle rang the doorbell three times
before I answered, my parents out for Audubon.
Under our yellow bug light in his plumber's suit,
he looked pretty sad: eyes raccoon tired,
cheeks unshaved, hands oil stained, nails black.
By now he'd whipped Chuckie with his belt.
"Is it girls?" he said. "Is that what's driving you kids nuts?"

I gave him an Irish coin squashed sharp and smooth,
not a word left on it when he spit and polished
with his sleeve. He tested the blade edge on his thumb
to see if it would cut. Mr Boyle eyed me darkly,
said, "If you were my boy, you'd know what I'd do."
"But I'm not," I said. The good coin that slipped off
the track and survived intact I kept, my token of kissing
Jill St. Clair the morning she brought Girl Scout cookies.
No one knew but the mailman who caught us.

Priceless

I tackled my brother in slo-mo
into the mothball smell of the chocolate
velvet couch with springs weaker

than Slinkies. He refused to fumble;
I threatened to bite his fingers
like a mad wolverine. "Stop roughhousing,"

Mom said, entering the rec room
for her eight o'clock show, *The Galloping
Gourmet*, with lipstick kisses

around her wineglass rim.
She never took notes, never made the recipes,
smiled too long at every joke,

saying, "That's priceless."
Afterward, she told me to pull the curtains.
"Our neighbors must think

we're running a nudist colony,"
she said, even though no one ever walked
naked in our house.

Drunk, she snored like a horse
upstairs in bed. My brother played Alfred Hitchcock,
smothering me with a couch pillow,

until I death-kicked free and decided to teach him
to drink wine in the basement. I checked the freezer
for the purple cow heart bearded with frost I'd won

in third-grade dissection. Mom kept every prize
we brought home, saying someday we'd thank her.
"You could put that heart in a new cow,

and it would still work," I said. "Would not,"
my brother said. What I really wanted to know
was why such a dumb animal had such a big heart.

We drank the sour wine and pissed
off the back porch under the yellow bug light.
Because he's fatter, my brother sprayed farther,

but he wasn't happy. "I hope the yard's dry
when Mom wakes up," he said. "Forget it," I said;
"dogs piss here all the time."

"Yeah, but she doesn't like them, either."

Easy Out

Jimmy Jags threw wicked curves,
sinkers, spitters, his secret crusher
that broke bones. I kicked dirt

on home plate, so the fat umpire bent
over with his tiny whisk broom, huffing
like a bulldog in his padded mask.

"Make him throw strikes," coach said.
"Easy out," shouted the catcher, waving in
the outfielders. I practiced my home run

swing three times, hammered the plate
with my bat, making it *oomph* with dust.
I looked up into the dark eyes of Jimmy Jags

ready to throw for my head. He belched,
loudest in the league, then spat a green wad
on the pitcher's mound like a dead 25 cent turtle.

When he wheeled with his pitch, I saw justice die.
The white moon flew kamikaze at my face.
"Stee-rike one!" the ump gloated.

I rose from my knees. The punks
behind the batter's cage flapped elbow wings
and bawked like chickens. "Watch the ball!"

coach pleaded. I hated this game.
All summer the bruised clouds refused to rain.
The grass tied to the field was tough as shoelaces.

The yellow dirt made my palms bleed with every slide.
This time I swung to kill Jimmy Jags for everything:
his shaving cuts and cigarette breath, his knuckle punches

in the halls, his girlfriends slurping sodas
for seven innings in the bleachers. They believed
he once peeled a baseball with his teeth.

I swung, but my knees went slack like fishing line
that just lost a great fish. The rising fastball smacked
the batter's cage, making the chain link sing.

Stuck, it glared like a grass-stained eye.
I tried religion. I promised God I'd mow the lawn
until autumn. I told Him what Jimmy Jags said about nuns.

This wicked curve spun for my face,
but I didn't flinch. I would smash the ball
into eternity, Jimmy Jags into oblivion.

"Next time," coach said, but didn't mean it.
The outfielders trotted for the bench, kicking
apart white dandelions.

"Hell, Jimmy Jags will spend his life pumping gas,"
Dad promised. I'm still looking every time I fill up.

Orthopedic

The first big word I hated as a boy:
the specter of fallen arches every time I stood
on the shoe store's measuring pad
and made an impression of muddy blue flats
where others left white bays.
The clerk threading laces in dog-brown shoes
told me astronauts had good feet—presidents, too.
He finished with polish and wooden shoe horns
I never used. Instead, I wore my orthopedics
for kicking skunk cabbages and squishing frog fart
bubbles from mud on my way to school.
The principal made me wash off with a janitor's hose
so I wouldn't track my anger from class to class.
Sneakers. Baseball cleats. Buffalo-hide cowboy boots
with pointed silver toes. I grew up to wear them all
through one phase or another, even bare feet
for summer camp in New Hampshire,
my calluses thick enough to tread on pine cones
and feel tickled. Flat feet hardly mattered,
long forgotten, until the morning
of my mother's funeral, when at 42
I learned I hadn't worn my fine Italian shoes
in so long, living at my mountain cabin
where work boots were the order of the day,
that mice had harvested my fine Italian laces
for their nests. Fortunately, my father,
a retired banker, had a closet of leather shoes.
Kneeling on his floor, I was surprised to discover
he hadn't used shoe horns, either. His dusty
Oxfords stiff as my old orthopedics
had laces studded with such tight and tiny knots
I was almost late untying them.

Blood Brothers

Remember the werewolf double feature
at the old porno theater on upper Broadway?
The seats had no room for our knees;
sticky paint covered gum barnacles.

We howled at the full moon slipping free
of bruised clouds, then the actors' faces growing
into wolf snouts with sounds like breaking furniture.
Their blue eyes kaleidoscoped into green.

They peed on hedges and hunted subway tunnels,
leaving shredded raincoats, a beggar's cup, teeth marks
on the turnstiles. By the office cooler the next morning,
they laughed at bloodstains on their tasseled loafers.

In the end they died from silver bullets
to the heart. Filing out, we discovered snow swirling
like torn pillow feathers. A cab tried to splash us with slush
and missed. We celebrated our new lives

in Manhattan by howling at the "Don't Walk" light
and walking. Within a year you moved home,
joined our father's timid life. You burned
pork chops, overboiled beans, made bowls of popcorn

that lasted into Letterman. You slept in fire engine sheets
in your boyhood bed, let the clock radio whisper
soft rock all night, as if you didn't trust
silent dreams. Your degrees

didn't matter. You worked the Christmas season
at the Post Office, rang bells for the Census, added blank years
to your resume. Maybe you were happy. I suffered
the hunger of wolves in Manhattan.

On My Block

The street trees wore Christmas lights year-round
like contorted angels.
The homeless man guarded his refrigerator box

with a trowel. Fire trucks answered false alarms.
Men in black raincoats
and yellow oxygen tanks waited

with axes. The parking meters wore
BROKEN hoods, window planters
grew Spanish weeds, and the pigeons

pranced like professional wrestlers,
waiting for their babushka lady's
stale crumbs. The teenage entrepreneur seated

on the fire hydrant sold twenty-five-cent cigarettes
to bums and yuppies trying to quit.
Rumor said he could also find you cheap tires.

One night the toothless man in the yellow vest
for "Dangerous Curves" caught me
at the "Don't Walk" light and whispered, "Hot oil,

these chicks will massage you down to the bone."
His eyes glistened like fried egg whites
because he had seen the glory

the way the crazies have always seen the glory
on these lost avenues.
I said, "Yes, take me to the angels."

We crossed to the block where a shattered moon
floated everywhere
in black windows, and the crickets

lording over abandoned lots sang
with the dry heat of downtown love.

Happy Hour

Empowered by Long Island ice teas
at the Rusty Scupper on Seventh Avenue,
we shouldered our bags and joined
the sidewalk parade of leather pirates
and homeless mystics pummeling
imaginary faces of God. The sunset ached
over New Jersey. The opera singer
with a starling's voice shook his tin cup
for nickels. Lethargic pigeons surrounded
a fire hydrant cryptic with graffiti.
Under a blue Salvation Army blanket
we found mannequin legs in ripped fishnets.
She wouldn't be safe here in the methadone district,
so we decided to take her home to a warm
apartment with cable and clean towels.
First we needed to find her lean and pouting
face, her nippleless chest, her fingers always reaching
for a stranger's cigarette. In the Dumpster
we vowed to make our love whole.
We tossed yesterday's newspapers high
into avenue updrafts to soar on crumpled wings.
We pranced on shredded-paper linguine
and discarded lettuce that smelled like bedding
after feverish dreams. We chased rats over the edge
and found rubbers discarded like unwanted fingers
from hospital gloves. The twilight stained
office towers with the blush of shame,
but we invented beauty with discarded wigs
and Styrofoam eyes. While our lovely mannequin
leaned her trim butt against the Dumpster
with toes pointed like a ballerina's,
we searched with giddy hearts beating
like butterflies nectaring
on the wanton flowers of the night.

Fucking Manhattan

Tireless, we ordered home delivery of diaphragm cream
by a sad Mexican boy under spastic lights
in your submarine-green hallway.
I tipped him $5, while you blew static hairs
off your favorite Marvin Gaye, hiccup-scratched
at college parties. With the volume lowered to a whisper,
so your psychotic neighbor wouldn't throw books
at her wall, we slow danced until I lasso-tossed
your nude bra onto a lamp, and you teethed
my nipples into tender cones.

For the final round, you wore maroon boots with gray
gum spots on the soles. I knelt to inhale
the scent down your spine to your ass, then
grabbed hips like bony handlebars and didn't stop,
vowing to outlast car alarms whooping and yenking,
the sports-bar drunks spilled on the avenue
chanting, "Go! Go! Go!"

Afterward, you offered Valium, but I preferred
to fall asleep naturally, meditating on striped kites
cast on the ceiling by street lamps through venetian blinds.
When shouting ruptured the alleyway, I peeked
through the blinds at a woman with red impatiens
on her fire escape hurling down a man's clothes:
khakis, loafers, white briefs that fell like a shot dove.
A naked man beside shackled garbage cans
caught his clothes one by one and yelled,
"Give me back my resume!"

I loved this scene. But you'd fallen asleep and stolen
my half of the covers for warmth against A/C.
To work off my excitement, I flipped on kitchen lights
to hunt roaches. But, smartly, you'd stashed all
our dirty dishes in the fridge for morning.
To be useful, I laid them in the kitchen bathtub
and sprayed scalding shower-nozzle water to scour
frozen grease. When your cat jumped from her radiator,

I noticed in the dark window across the alleyway
an orange cigarette tip drawing a curious circle,
the woman with impatience watching me
naked and hardening in the greatest city on Earth.

The Philosophy of Margaritas

Two slushy green drinks in ice cream sundae
glasses, and your friend with her new blonde hair spiky
as winter thistle locked mouths with a stranger,
as if kissing was a contest like sucking
the most from an orange. The wiggly hands
of the Mickey Mouse clock clapped
at midnight. "Thunder Road" hit
the juke box a third time. I grabbed
your small hand hard as chicken bones
for such a comforting body, and we burst
into the frigid night to breathe cold daggers
at icicled street lamps under the Hoboken moon.

We swung our unzipped coats like superhero capes.
You raised both arms as if signaling touchdown,
and leaned to the left, leaned to the right,
your new aerobicize for sexier stomach muscles.
I karate-kicked a telephone pole, plopped
on a garbage bag for a bean-bag chair,
and admired a wooden television console
with golden fabric on stereo speakers dumped
like an altarpiece in tomorrow's curbside trash.

Hours after bedtime in Yankees PJs, I remembered,
I watched a TV like this one when Neil Armstrong bound
across the moon, an astronaut on Planet Trampoline.
Dad said, "I bet he could hit a hell of golf shot."
Mom said, "Please." Dad said, "A *heck* of a golf shot."
Mom said she'd never live on a planet with so much dust.
In those days when Mom and Dad still talked, I believed
when my rocket trip came, I'd be skipping the moon and Mars,
shooting past Jupiter. I'd be racing for the stars.

College Daze

On Halloween to wear my frog mask to her party,
recite her favorite Robert Creeley
in her doorway, before she recognized me as me.

To blend passion fruit daiquiris in her Waring,
juggle peanuts high enough to catch them one-by-one
in my acrobatic mouth. To sword fight

with salted pretzel sticks her premed boyfriend,
majoring in Eliot, Yeats and Pound. To declare victory,
blowing out the paper tongues from party favors,

then pluck the college football song on a ukulele,
substituting *Flintstones* lyrics in a mousy
nitrous oxide voice, thanks to a Cool Whip nozzle.

To swim her pool length underwater in my jeans
and frog mask gone completely foggy, nearly crack
my forehead at the end, but still have breath

to swim back and shark-attack the naked legs
treading water—oops, her mother's
nightly exercise. To swamp the rubber ducky.

To throw my clothes into her dryer, select
a black spaghetti strap from her bedroom closet,
pinched across my stomach, but otherwise attractive.

To candle-light one of her clove cigarettes,
tap my ashes in a demitasse, and disagree with her professor
re: the metrics of fucking in e.e. cummings.

To wonder why he's curious about my bloody knee,
until I notice the damage for myself. It would be frightening
if I hadn't done the same last week on my bike.

To scrape her metal garden rake in circles on the road,
spinning until the ring of sparks connects:
a burning snake swallowing its tail.

To grow so dizzy I land sideways on her lawn,
watch the moon revolve slowly
back into its rightful place.

All this, and she thought I was stoned.
But I knew love was a double-hearted dynamo
even on half a gram and poetry.

During the Yankees' August Slump

Fucking Squazzi, he pulled over on Park Avenue and grabbed
his dad's favorite driving iron from the trunk to swing
at a cabby's grill for stopping at yellow.
We showed up an hour late for rugby against Prudential
Bache loaded with ex-cons from the mailroom.
Our side was down two tries and a concussion;
a tornado watch threatened from New Jersey.
My first scrimmage, I blacked out under the pileup,
so they dumped ice water on my face and laid me
on the sideline to study glassine caterpillars
crawling on the sky. I hated the financial league.
Squazzi yelled, "Yo, Pussy" and elbowed some teeth.
The fight started after Spike got head-butted and squirted
his nose like puttanesca sauce. I got one good shot at a knee

and woke up in an EMS truck with my intravenous bag
swinging like hurricane ship rigging. The driver
horn-blasted traffic and cursed cops in Spanish.
The medic pressed my fingernails white,
said I was dehydrated from tequila shots last night.
Silenced in an oxygen mask, I saw a blood minnow
swim up my intravenous tube and wished I could wake up
in Connecticut and go sailing like I was supposed to,
before Squazzi showed. Riding shotgun, he called
the driver a faggot for voting Pedro Martinez an All-Star.

I woke up under blue lights buzzing like patio zappers
in the emergency hall beside a mummy face
with more tubes up its nose than a distributor cap.
Squazzi got booted for pinching a nurse.
I couldn't talk anyway with my tongue dried out,
my brain reeling from weird dreams after every minute
of sleep. All the doctors did was order more intravenous,
until I had to piss in my gurney. The nurse
handed me a bent-necked bottle I filled like a horse,
my stream echoing down the hall. The intercom
announced a chaplain's call on line three.

That night I didn't find Squazzi until 10:30 at Rusty's
in Times Square, running 32,000 points on topless pinball
after his first blow job upstairs. The bartender with eyes
soaked in Bloody Marys saw my hospital bracelet
and said, "You guys have been coming in all night.
They letting you out on some kind of holiday?"
I shrugged on my stool. All I wanted was to catch the Yankees'
late night at Seattle over peanuts and watered beer.
Squazzi missed three spares on the table-bowling machine,
demanded fresh table wax by sliding his empty mug
down the bar to collide with a hooker's Manhattan
and sequin purse. The bartender raised a Louisville Slugger.
Squazzi and I stepped outside under the golden marquee
of cocktail dancers with cherry nipples and tried
to remember where he'd parked his father's car.

The Television Stays on Until the End

So this lady, she's wearing pink bunny slippers and night cream,
hugging her tabby and shooing a sidewalk crazy
who warns God doesn't live in her doorway anymore.
Bobby double-parks our moving van, tells her Dominican super
we'll just be a minute. But already he spots a Brownie
down the block chalking tires, so I follow her alone
up stairs stinking of fried plantains. Back in Ohio
they think this city is pure David Letterman.
They wonder why I'm not acting in commercials,
at least. They don't understand, this lady arm-tucks
her tabby like a fullback and doesn't stop
until her fifth-floor door with a fisheye for visitors.
The whole way up I stare at her elbow bruised like a tornado.

She tells me, last night her boyfriend smoked a glass pipe
that stank like burning tires. The suicide hot line
advised her to move out. Now he gets back in an hour
from a Gypsy cab shift, and he carries three kinds of knives
from the Islands. She starts bawling, slipping drool
down her chin. I hand her my bandanna
with yesterday's sweat and windshield swipes.
I should tell her, speed is our specialty
like our laundromat flier says, but I wonder,
why does every morning start like this:
Wednesday's drag queen threatening lawsuits
for a broken heel, Tuesday's crackhead slapping her baby.
Why won't my agent get off his ass and book auditions
for once, quit telling me I've got the perfect face for comedy.

Like every emergency call, she hasn't boxed anything herself:
not stereo speakers topped with kingdoms of melted candles,
or the velvet Jesus with blue eyes and black lashes
doing a poor job of hiding a water stain. I dump my box flats
on the floor, ask for newspaper stuffing. She apologizes
for getting hysterical and opens her fridge for a Colt .45
20-ounce can she rubs on her temples. Then she flops
on a green recliner. She wouldn't be bad-looking

if she combed her rat's nest and didn't advertise
her dimpled thighs by letting her blue bathrobe part
over her knees. She asks if I've seen her cigarettes.
"Lady," I say, "are you going to help?
We've got 55 minutes until the knives come home."

She asks, "Why are you wearing Yankees batting gloves?"
Maybe it's the humidity, or the charred pipe in the ashtray,
or Bobby pounding out a heart attack on the horn,
but I don't have the patience. I tell the truth.
"My brother plays center field." So there,
I'm the O'Brien to feel sorry for, the guy to bum
free stadium tickets. So ask me, "Did you get hurt?
Is that why you're the side guy on a cheap moving van?"
But she doesn't. "I love your American baseball,"
she says. "Your men look so cute in those uniforms.
And they get so passionate when they strike out."
Pressing her remote, she pets her tabby
and tells me, the television stays on until the end.
She and the cat need the soothing voice of Kathie Lee.
Doesn't matter. I just quit.

Masters of the Game
--*Norwalk, Connecticut*

All four courts always empty at the Norwalk Y,
we picked the second for the loudest sneaker squeaks
and biggest bounces off the rear Plexiglas
permanently smudged by our hands and racquets.
This game wasn't tennis, with prissy scores
and boundary lines. Every shot remained in play,
no matter how it rattled off the ceiling light bulb cage
or ricocheted off an elbow, foot, or head.
Racquetball guaranteed an hour of sweat and cursing,
burning lungs and miraculous returns,
an hour so much finer than anything at work
those long months at an environmental magazine
with plunging circulation and writers suing to get paid.

Over time we mastered submarine shots,
towering three-walled returns, and, nastiest of all,
the gentle lob that glanced the front wall
and died in tiny dribbles. Hell, we were good,
getting great. How, then, did I manage such a stunt?
Jammed against the Plexiglas, I tightly swung
an over-the-shoulder return and somehow paddle-
whacked my teeth. My tongue confirmed my stupidity;
my front tooth sharp and angled as a guillotine.
It didn't hurt, but I felt such sadness I wouldn't leave
my hands and knees, searching the varnished floor
for my lost half-tooth camouflaged by polish.
At last I knew I had to quit this fucking job.

The Waiting Room

He'd really done it to himself this time, already good
for two heart attacks, walking pneumonia, a colon scare,
and now choking on gristle at Smith & Wollensky's.

They gurneyed him past gauzy faces and screamers,
sent me to the waiting room where Hassids left latkes stains
on magazines. Chuck Scarborough on News 4

had too much orange in his face. Sarah arrived with *People*,
her Prozac for waiting rooms. It was true: Crisis
made you horny. I wanted to hide my fingers in her blonde curls,

rub noses with her new freckles from roof tanning. She flipped
pages. "You're so anxious, why don't you go to the movies?"
"My father could be dead," I said, "and I'm going to eat popcorn?"

"He won't die from Beef Wellington," she said.
"You don't know my old man," I replied.
"He punctured his eardrum trying to stab a fly

with his keys." She offered cinnamon sugarless gum.
Instead, I followed a hospital gown rolling his IV stand
outside for a cigarette, bummed two for myself,

and remembered a papaya stand down the avenue
near the porno district. After ten blocks, I wondered
if I had the wrong street. An old Kung Fu Palace showed

The Six-Fingered Hand of Death. I studied the poster,
puzzled by which finger was fake.
A guy in a blue delivery shirt exited the glass door.

"Phil?" I said, my old man's name stitched in red. "Phil?"
he grunted. "Your shirt." He glanced down like he didn't know.
"I got it at St. Patty's rummage store." Turning uptown,

I inspected a dusty window with pink blowup dolls,
wondered who will finally clean out the old man's closet.
The army uniform with mothballs in the pockets, wingtips

with knotted laces, joke ties collected for parties.
As a boy, I hid in his woolly darkness when he called me
for church. Wearing his stiff shoes, I smelled shaving cream

dried on collars and found pennies, ticket stubs, and breath mints
deep in his pockets. I wondered how much he cared
when a woman's perfume got on his clothes. He tempted me

with the smell of frying bacon, but I stood straight
in his army jacket heavy to my knees, and watched the crack
of door light for his shadow, afraid to sneeze.

Elegy for a Pessimist

The funeral home shaved him neater than he shaved himself,
trimmed the mousy bush inside his nose,
found a college tie without stains,
and shut his eyes snug as peanut shells
for an attitude of serenity he never found at home.
The father I knew prowled all night in a tartan bathrobe
with a dampened pipe spilling in his pocket
and calfskin slippers worn to nurse his ingrown nails.
He fretted and cursed about such matters as where in hell
he'd left his *Economic Review* analysis of 1966,
now being baldly plagiarized by some young prick at MIT.
Alas, in that house stacked past the windows
with data printouts and yellowing Treasury reports,
he rarely uncovered what he needed.
Stoking up his pipe, he vowed to sue the dean as well,
then terrified the sofa cat by igniting
the can of paper trash with his burning match.
Not until 4 a.m. did he sink in his recliner for a fitful nap,
waking in fury at 5:30 if the delivery man
tossed *The New York Times* too loudly on his porch.

A genius, the obituaries unanimously agreed:
my father had predicted five of the last six recessions
to the month, making his investment clients wealthy in bonds
and precious metals. Our Senator sent condolences.
The bank president gave a heartfelt eulogy,
calling my father the most honest economist he'd ever met.
"This man never tried to sell you sunshine," the banker said,
"but he made damn sure you were ready for a hurricane."
So many dignitaries filing past his casket
slipped me business cards with private numbers,
they must have figured I'd taken up my father's business.

After his cremation I was surprised by the lightness
of his ashes. He left me free to scatter them
where I wished: a decision harder than expected.
Had he been a sailor or mountaineer,
I could have cast him on an ocean or icy summit.

But an economist? A filing cabinet
hardly seemed appropriate. To ponder this dilemma,
I decided to mow the lawn grown wild with dandelions
since his hospitalization. From the garage
I rolled out the squeaky mower, remembering he paid me
a quarter per quarter acre as a teen, vowing
to teach his spoiled son the true value of a dollar.
Now, as I rammed the mower into the green morass,
it nearly choked, then spat its way clear
with wads of shredded grass
in a triumphant cloud of violet smoke.
I trimmed by the hedge, mowed flag stripes
up and down the low slope, recovered teenage reveries
of becoming famous as a Hollywood screenwriter,
until, abruptly, the rotor blade grounded
on a flat stump wigged with weeds
that had stopped me countless times. In the stalled quiet
I saw three robins already hunting worms in the fresh-cut grass.
I wondered: How would they like the taste of ash?

The Fish Are Laughing

We'd taken a Caribbean vacation for sex,
but the camp peacock begging on our cottage steps
distracted me. He bobbed his warty face,
expecting food on my palm, but I didn't trust him

not to pluck at my eyes. I tossed trail mix
down the boardwalk, watched him prance away
on clownish chicken feet, his tail sweeping the planks
like a gown. You poured tiny sugar piles on a porch railing

for yellow bananaquits that flew back to the trees
with white crystals on their beaks, as if gorging on cocaine.
By now the turquoise bay beckoned with sunken clouds
of coral reefs. We found the rental shack and the beach dude

with sun-whitened hair, trying to match flipper pairs,
drenched in pot perfume. He tightened your mask straps,
making you feel claustrophobic with such a snug fit.
You wondered how many strangers had breathed

in your snorkeling tube. "Okay," I said, "find a stupid
beach book." You smiled, "I didn't know I was swimming
with a shark." The rental dude chuckled, slipping
your perfect arches into blue flippers. I regretted

not starting with sex, but we'd paid $20 for this crappy
equipment. We walked through mangroves, where mud crabs
pattered like rain, scurrying down holes with a final wink
of their pink claws. On the hot, loose sand

fleas besieged my ankles. I pulled on my flippers
and drifted under the calm water's cellophane ceiling.
I kicked the lethargic brown rags of bottom plants.
A green turtle shifted in the silt like a manhole cover

come to life. It stroked with curved paws until its head
floated like a reptilian tennis ball in flaming yellow
and black. Now I knew this vacation was worth
every penny. When I looked back, you stood in shallows,

yanking off flippers. You said your feet had cramped,
your mask had filled like an aquarium, you'd almost drowned
in four feet of water like in a goddamned Woody Allen movie.
When I smiled, you said, "I hope the fish are laughing, too."

Suddenly, a pelican crashed like a box kite
in the hard water behind me. I heard every bone break
in my ignorance of the world.

Quaker Hill

After hellos among my fiancee's family and cousins,
I slipped away from her grandmother's pool party
into the woods with my first field guides.
Hours later I returned to describe my discoveries:
a wood thrush wore mascara dribbled down its chest,
a warbler sang squeaky as a bicycle wheel
in a sassafras tree, jewelweed seeds tasted of almonds,
hickory nuts made my hands smell of lemons.
The greatest treasure was a sixty-foot chestnut tree,
a rarity eighty years after a catastrophic blight.
Catkins flowered on its green canopy like clusters
of foot-long fingers dressed for a wedding.
An American Lady butterfly fluttered nearby.

A decade later when her grandmother died,
my wife and I closed the country house one weekend.
We emptied dusty liquor bottles down the drain
that smelled like mouthwash. We swept dead bees
off bookshelves. Saturday, we were busy with the plumber,
real estate agent, and negligent lawn service that let
the grass grow a foot and seed with dandelions.
We hardly had time to visit her neighbor, tending
his beehives, pouring a tin can of smoke to calm
bees inside. Last year's hives produced no honey,
he said. The queen had been too weak.

Sunday morning, I woke early and watched a doe and fawn
graze as I finished my coffee. While my wife slept,
I slipped into the woods a final time, surprised
by dozens of mushrooms: white parasols, violet caps,
orange trumpets, red amanitas sprinkled with flakes
like granola. I picked samples: a pancake-brown boletus,
an old-man-of-the-woods scaly as a pine cone,
Indian Pipes like miniature candle-wax saxophones.
On the kitchen table I arranged them by color and shape
for my wife to admire this strange kingdom of life.
But waking for coffee, she complained she felt nauseated
at seeing these slimy things like an alien's organs,
at seeing me play so fondly with death.

Dead Wasps, Black Trees, Sugar Stars

Dead wasps lay like peanut shells on dusty windowsills
in the country house after your father died. I snorted coke,
flossed, swept up the crispy insects with an old *Economist*,
his favorite magazine. I snapped the blue quilt three times
until it settled squarely on the bed. Your shins felt cold,
your hips stiff as a wooden bowl. Kneeling into you,
my knees hurt from the plywood under the mattress
for his bad back. You whispered for me to relax, slow down,
think about baseball, whatever men did as women caught up.

I said, "I feel lucky; let's go out and look for meteors."
But you chose ratty slippers, your mother's heavy bathrobe.
You tossed logs onto the fire, causing orange sparks to flock
up the chimney. I donned three pairs of socks and wrapped
a scarf around my neck until my head rode a woolen brace.

I stepped into the frozen night with runny moonlight spilled
across the hard shell of snow scratched by my earlier experiments
on skis. I climbed the white hillside scribbled with straw grass,
past the black apple tree. My boots punched loud footprints,
then loosened rocks, as I hopped a stone wall. At the crest
the flag spruce grew branches to the east. A breeze teased
weed stalks to drop their snow fingers. It took blind luck
to spot a meteor, so I admired the sugaring of stars,
the blinking jet pulling a smoky contrail of moonlight.
The passengers tucked warmly behind their windows—
I wondered if they knew they were missing heaven.

Batting for the Dead

In 1925, Hart Crane, a young poet having a hard time in Manhattan, spent the summer helping a friend restore a farmhouse in the rural hills of upstate New York. Their Fourth of July party was a memorable weekend. "Nothing could beat the hilarity of this place," Crane wrote his mother. "--with about an omnibusful of people here from New York and a case of gin, to say nothing of jugs of marvelous hard cider from a neighboring farm . . . We went swimming at midnight, climbed trees, played blind man's bluff, rode in wheelbarrows, and gratified every caprice for three days." In 1930, he published his masterpiece, The Bridge, *an epic poem about America. Alas, two years later he jumped off a ship, ending his tumultuous life. But the Fourth of July party continues.*

To E.S., my former wife and lasting friend.

Seventy years ago Hart Crane played this game.
It's an uphill field with a stone pitcher's mound
and a crab apple tree in shallow center,
which your grandmother once climbed as a child,
until a pop fly pinballed down and blackened her eye.
No one remembers how well Hart Crane hit or threw,
but he saddled the young girl on his shoulders
and galloped back to the barbecue
for watermelon and buttered ears of corn.
Now, she's dead, too.

What a team: the dead.
The teenagers taking the field
may know the nonchalant trot of the televised professionals,
the suave way to blow gum bubbles between pitches,
the taunting cadence of the "swing-batter, swing-batter" chants.
It's the metaphysics of the game they don't understand.
Consider the lineup:

Your grandfather, a mural painter
blacklisted as a social realist then rediscovered
as a Freudian symbolist, an old master
of busty landscapes and phallic smokestacks.

Suffering MS, his legs as slack as dying codfish,
he drove his electric cart full tilt after a surprising hit,
until the rodent pit between second and third
stopped his wheel, spinning up dirt.
Tagged out by a throw with wet leaves still attached,
he saluted with a draw from his flask
and quoted Salvador Dali on the sex life of clouds.

Your spinster aunt with a good-luck dandelion
tucked behind her ear once popped a homer
over the stone wall slumped in right.
She promptly retired to her watercolors
for twenty years. As a retired nurse from P.S. 75,
she handed out butterfly Band-Aids
to all the children who scratched themselves,
chasing fouls into rose vines.

Your uncle, the sociologist, always bunted.
His bitter stories about tenure we didn't understand,
nor the way he suffered writer's block
by sneaking afternoons in an uptown porno theater.
But his brother, the architect, spit on his hands
for a tighter bat grip. He hammered the first pitch
into the neighbor's bull pasture, trotted
the bases with his broken handle raised like a torch:
a wooden mushroom in place of a flame.
Of course I could go on:
Lefties, switch-hitters, mistresses in fishnet stockings
your great-aunt proudly ignored.
She kept score in Russian.

The newest member is your father,
passed last autumn, the Anarchist of Second Base.
For forty years he guarded the bag
with his glass eye and gritty, squinting smile.
So what if he lost easy pop-ups in the sun?
Nobody made it around second without tripping
or hearing a nasty aside about Rockefeller.

Granted, he wasn't much of an athlete:
he didn't hike, swim, or ride his Exercycle
prescribed after the by-pass. With his ghostly legs
and tangled veins, he came from Russian peasant stock
impervious to sunshine and exercise, or so he claimed.
But he always turned out for the game.
He wore his Depression boyhood glove,
still oiled the pocket softer than a baby's cheek,
or so he said with a wink. To us his antique mitt
looked like a swollen bear paw.
Between innings children wore it as a hat.

In college he'd studied mill workers sewing baseballs,
and renounced the game in solidarity.
But after a Ph.D. in labor economics, he'd mellowed
as a bank senior vice president who supported Democrats.
Still, on the field, he played by rules not found in any book.
Should an easy catch pop out of his glove
like a magic trick dove, he lunged to catch it again,
and if he did, announced a double play.
No, your father didn't have a golden glove,
but he knew where his true talents lay;
in the final inning he loudly recited
"Casey at the Bat" in Yiddish
to make the other side strike out laughing.

When the game came down to a prayer,
your father always batted cleanup.
He alone had the brains to outwit the pitcher,
your great-uncle, the jazz curmudgeon,
who wrote nasty notices for *The Partisan Review*
and sipped Scotch from his infield glass
between strikeouts. A tyrant on the mound,
he had a repertoire of trick pitches, which he dubbed
the Beiderbecke Express, the Teagarden Curve,
the Pee Wee Russell Changeup, and Bobby Hackett Heater.
To be honest, they all looked the same,
a softball lofted slow and fat as a harvest moon,

until the batter swung and saw the pitch
drift past his bat weightless as a dandelion seed.

Your father took the plate as if the Cold War
would be reenacted. The two men glared,
traded insults quoted from Trotsky and Podhoretz,
argued the legality of every pitch's spin.
Of course, they were really playing the great game
of patience. At last, the ball might slip,
lazy and unspun, from your great-uncle's hand.
He rushed off the mound as if to grab it back,
while your father fixed his good eye on the pitch,
then belted a rainbow over the crab apple tree,
or lined a rocket through the outfield daisies,
or fouled a monster over the barn into the chicken pen.
Or missed by a foot, fanning up dust
that clouded the plate and made the catcher sneeze.

Afterward, the two retired to the barbecue.
Your father grilled tofu dogs to save his arteries,
while your great-uncle switched to cider and lamented
nobody read his old friend Hart Crane anymore.

Now my turn has come to pinch-hit for the dead.
The new pitcher is a young fashion editor
in black tights and tennis visor. She sips
Evian and wears wrist bands for a drier grip.
The rumor is she's unbeaten for her company team
in the Central Park publishing league.
But I remember some things your father said:
the future belongs to the Chinese,
vermouth ruins martinis,
most editors are callous bastards,
and nobody has written better poems than Hart Crane.
The first pitch I connect.
The softball sails into the tangle
of the crab apple tree, where a new girl sits,
dreaming of weddings and crickets.

The Snake at the End

She didn't want to watch
the black snake uncoiling its wetness
on the laurel branch.

I insisted and lifted the four-foot skin
clear as fingernail onto the end
of my walking stick to admire the scales
from tail rings to belly planks to eyelid bubbles.
The nose wore the mark of a wishbone.

She found it repulsive
that I carried this souvenir on my stick
as eagerly as a boy with a baseball pennant
all the way down Slide Mountain
to decorate my new cabin.

She left before
I draped the skin on my stone mantelpiece,
expanding the still life display
of chalky deer bones, birch bark scrolls,
pine cones, and the red sumac flower
standing in a vase like a velvet microphone.

After a month she filed papers,
and the snakeskin smelled like a wet dog.
Now I was beginning to learn how things decay,
but not always for the worse. The mushroom that melted
overnight into a black puddle on my journal table
varnished the wood with an odor of licorice
I hadn't savored since childhood.

Insomnia

-- Platte Clove, Catskills

History has failed to record the mice
who nested in Rip Van Winkle's beard,
or the stinging nettles that grew
for twenty summers between his rotting shoes.
While Rip snored, chipmunks stashed
acorns in his pockets, and spotted salamanders
wiggled safely for generations
beneath his back. Once
a bear tripped over his chest
and stopped to eat his pipe.
Wood toads hopped
along his buttons, and oven birds
sang *Tea-cher, Tea-cher, Tea-cher,*
in his ears all summer without prompting
any nightmares. When Rip woke
and wandered back to town
with a rusty gun muzzle
and ten-inch fingernails,
he became America's first great celebrity
of sleep, a cautionary tale
of life without a snooze alarm.

Tonight I lay awake and listen to thunder
echo in the clove like bowling pins
bouncing off cliffs. In lightning
white curtains flash like the ghosts
of children I never had.
The old maple tree blusters
helplessly in the storm. I wonder
how Rip managed to forget his unpaid bills,
his sullen boy, and bitter wife,
who didn't look up from the butter churn,
when he closed the door
to lead his dog up the mountain
for an afternoon of hunting squirrels.
He lay down for a moment long enough to sleep
through his mortgage. I'd settle

for twenty minutes without a mental Post-It note.
I'm a stunning success at staying awake
and lamenting my lost chances.
I visualize myself as a rotting log
and begin counting toads on my chest moss.
I wonder how Rip stumbled
across the secret of human hibernation,
a trick so wonderful I've paid to watch it
in movies about people traveling to the stars.

The Life of the Stag
-- Catskills

You nibbled sharply on my lips, testing,
"You just want a girlfriend to help you carry logs."
I held you bony and damp in my lap,
studied the cheek mole you said children loved to touch.
"And go to the movies with," I said.
Your black Manhattan jeans lay dropped
on the fire rug by my rubber-soled Wolverines.
Smoke leaked from the wood stove like a cigarette.

In the morning we snowshoed Cross Mountain.
I showed you beech trees graffitied by bear claws
the size of our hands, and told you my story:
after the Hoboken divorce, I chose these mountains,
hung a Cherokee mask by my door,
filled my pencil holder with wild turkey feathers,
wrote my first ode to porcupines.

Then I found my Inner Wendigo,
named after the Indian spirit in a low-budget movie
shot one winter by our reservoir.
Half-deer loaded with antlers like bone chandeliers,
half-human in buckskin leggings,
this creature hurdled like an Olympian
through the midnight forest, while strobe lights
flashed beech trees, fierce as totem poles.
"And what was the Wendigo chasing?" you asked.
"The same old story," I said, "revenge."
We kissed, turning me back into a man.

The White Hawk of Rosendale

(By age 44, Thoreau was dying of tuberculosis.)

For my 44th, my girlfriend proposed we search
for the white hawk of Rosendale, a nifty idea,
if I hadn't already prowled those roads and knocked
on doors to ask about an albino by the corn fields.
The wary residents answered with the coldness
I'd met at 17, pitching vacuums door-to-door.
Some didn't even know Rosendale had hawks.

A backyard birder, my girlfriend didn't understand
we'd be chasing a ghost, but I didn't dare disappoint her.
On my birthday morning we bundled for the blue
December weather and parked beside the field
of frosted stubble sparkling with sunlit ice.
Passing trucks whipped us with arctic gusts.
We hopped the guardrail, descended into cattails
by a marsh ditch with autumn leaves frozen clear in ice.
With binoculars I scanned distant trees and couldn't believe
our dumb luck—perched on the biggest sycamore,
blatant as a lighthouse beam! The white-chested hawk
spoiled everything, coasting down on dark wings.

By 44, Thoreau was dying. I felt I was failing, too.
What could I say? I'd lived in my cabin three years longer
than he did at Walden, published my first chapbook
with a minimum of typos, paid my bills promptly
since July. I had freelance work and a girlfriend.
Yet Thoreau found time to hone a million words
into brilliant aphorisms and still walk four hours a day.
I kept getting stuck waiting for the FedEx truck.

By now my girlfriend had chilly fingers in her gloves,
so we returned over the guardrail toward the car.
She spotted something above the telephone pole.
"Look in the tree," she said. "Is that your bird?"
All I saw was a plastic bag snagged like thousands
I'd seen in 16 years of Hoboken and Manhattan,
the life I'd come to the mountains to escape.

Then wings opened white as wedding gowns.
No mistaking it for a gull or ferocious pigeon:
a true hawk, it circled with jerky turns, slow
and curious, kiting the wind with luminous wings.
Joined by the second hawk tipping its red tail,
the albino hovered, a pair profiled against blue sky.
"If only we had a camera," my girlfriend said.
"We'd make a fortune from this picture."
But this priceless gift was my first sighting
of a mortal and its angel guardian.

Reintroduce Elk to the Catskills, Please

Stuck all morning on my letter-to-the-editor.
What more can I say? Elk have eyes the color of earth,
neck ruffs like Chinese scholars' beards.
But I know the newspaper wants real reasons,
and my girlfriend wants my computer to search the Web
for baked-pumpkin recipes. Snuggled downstairs
on my cabin couch, she laughs again
at her Carl Hiaasen mystery. This time, a minor character
worries his penis is shrinking from steroids.
Six times a day, she reads me aloud,
he ducks into bathrooms with measuring tape.
I don't really laugh. I have such disquieting thoughts.
Osama bin Laden is four months younger than me.
Last Christmas my ex-wife considered suicide.
By my age Kerouac had already died.
Why not give the elk a chance?

End of the Country Love Story

The morning after our walk around Walden Pond,
I noticed your driveway gravel littered with peach pits
rubbed gray by our tires coming and going,
our busy autumn of poetry festivals and museum trips.

How we'd admired the absurd abundance
of your small peach tree, its limbs gradually splitting
under the fragrant weight of hundreds and hundreds
of spotted peaches firm as crab apples. The two
you'd picked in August hadn't twisted softly off their pits
like store-bought peaches. You'd sliced them
into hard-won smiles garnishing our cereal.
Their sweetness was like nothing we'd ever tasted,
a sweetness heralding an autumn of peach pies
and cobblers, preserves, and cranking
the antique farm bucket for peach ice cream.

But the frosted lawn this morning made me wonder
what Thoreau would have written of our neglected promise,
our squandered harvest ground into driveway gravel.

A Delivery from Ikea

For the week after she announced
she'd quit using birth control
or I could move out,
the long white CD cabinet
delivered from Ikea
lay on her living room floor,
awaiting her friend
to help mount it by the couch,
a glass-lidded casket
I stepped over many times,
accused by the emptiness inside.

The Shout

-- Overlook Mountain, Catskills

The obese moon lit a pewter path
through ridgeline oaks black as goblins,
chalky birches like an audience of ghosts.
Windows at the hotel ruins framed constellations
with names I'd forgotten. The summit cabin
wore icy fangs, a padlock caked in frost.

On clifftop rocks I sat on chiseled names
from romances old as hotel ruins.
With a blanket wrapped round my knees
I enjoyed the panorama: the golden brooch
of Woodstock's lights, the silver-snaking Hudson,
the hunchbacked headless Catskills
huddled to the west.

As a boy I never learned how to yodel,
so now I shouted, "Yabba Dabba Doo!"
Then listened, listened.
Not even an echo.
My ex in Manhattan this New Year's Eve.

Winter Blues
-- *The Catskills*

Grumbling up the road,
   the snowplow
      guilt-trips me to shovel.

Shoving open the cabin door,
   I catch the red squirrel
      pop-eyed at the feeder,

a prisoner inside the squirrel-proof cage.
   Yet it squeezes free,
      scrambles up the hemlocks,

shaking off skeleton bones of snow
   that land *oomph* like pillows.
      Is it too much to hope

for redpolls, instead? Should I be satisfied
   with an escape artist who chatters
      incessantly?

The plow descends, spinning yellow lights
   and spreading sand
      like a trailing gown.

I'll shovel tomorrow. For now I throw
   snowballs at the feeder,
      honing my aim.

Sweat Lodge

Fire-heated sacred stones crowd the pit
in the sweat lodge framed with saplings,
roofed with blankets. Sage flakes
sprinkled on the rocks twice ignite
like candle flames, revealing our circle
of folded knees. Someone blows them out.

A ladled splash lifts stone dust in steam
to clog my nose. The second bursts my skin
with sweat. Stones split to share strength
held strong a million years. Sorrows
uncage from my bones. In the pit
the Earth's core glows molten orange.

Do you remember the haloed moon
above mountain ridges one New Year's Eve?
Where you saw rainbow rings, I saw only white,
blind to all but stars and forest darkness.
Now the moon inside my chest I exchange
for a glowing stone: this heart forged in fire.

Tricking the Stars
--Route 28, Catskills

Driving home late and exhausted, I tried Christian radio
on a lark, learned about the washing of feet,
until trooper lights spun cross-eyed in my rearview.
The female officer had a face I'd trust for a babysitter,
a black flashlight John would have died for.

But John lay in a nursing home bed with a gauze scarf
and plastic breathing tube, doing all he could do
to open his blue eyes and close them. After 16 months
on a pillow, his lips had sunken from atrophy,
his lower swollen out like bumper,

his upper thinned and tucked under the bumper.
His wife treated him to straw drops of root beer,
his childhood favorite. John did all he could do
not to lose them. Dribbles on his lips
threatened to slide down his gray whiskers.

On each cabin visit John brought a new flashlight.
He knew I had the darkness to experiment.
Outside we aimed beams at stars and once or twice
caught flickers back. I told the officer just once
she should let the speed limit be 68.

Miles

To be so cool forty years later
Allen Murphy still reveres
the way you said "shit,"
not "shoot" with a bite,
not some hapless whine about fate,
but "shit" like a whip-crack
aimed so precisely
from your night club chair
only Allen Murphy heard it;
Allen, a hayseed in Cleveland at 19,
come to hear your Quintet with his dad,
thinking maybe on his way to the men's room
he'll slide by your table. "Shit,"
said so well, Allen Murphy pops out
of my living room chair forty years later
to reenact every nervous step,
closer and closer,
until you gave the word.
Miles, you fucker, you genius,
you taught Allen Murphy how to say "shit."
Now he rules every inch of the room.

The Pistachio Question

What I wanted to know was the rest of the story Jack started to tell years ago about standing naked in a woman's high heels in her closet then farting loudly, as she tried to explain the bedside cocaine to her husband . . .

But Jack was married now, toweling his hair in all directions. His wife poured coffee, while their seven-year-old scrawled fierce grass with the stub of a crayon.

"Lilly, did you ask Will about bears?"

Jack had visited my cabin, reminded of his own years in the mountains, where, like me, he always pissed off the porch and never cared about curtains.

Lilly ignored him to draw monkeys.

"How did you sleep?" asked his wife, worried their futon unfolded too close to the window for a country visitor in Park Slope.

"Fine," I said. "For an alarm clock, I heard a house finch sing in your hedge."

"Is that who that is?" She whistled the song as well as the finch itself, a bubbling series of squeaks.

"Do you want to see my bird?" Lilly asked.

"No. You've got to get dressed for soccer." Not just her father, Jack was also her coach.

"My family loves birds," his wife said. "My dad, a professor, wrote all his books with Sinbad, the parrot, perched on his head. The bird made sure Dad didn't get up before he finished five pages."

"His name is Pistachio," said Lilly, carrying the cage like a watchman's lantern much big for a child. The green-bellied bird rocked on its wooden bar, shuffling its feet and flicking its tail. Its yellow forehead looked soft as a thumb. When Lilly lowered the cage to the floor, the bird took a swipe at the face in its mirror.

"His favorite food is pistachios," she said. "But we save those for Christmas and birthdays. Last night we clipped his wings. It didn't hurt. His feathers are like fingernails."

"Lilly, we've got ten minutes. You can't play midfield in your PJs," Jack said. "Honey, have you seen my whistle?"

"Did you look on top of the dryer?" his wife asked. "In the bowl with your watch and pocket change?"

"Lilly, I said don't."

Her cupped hands brought forth her bird. It exploded into sputtering flight, barely climging, fighting to rise on stubby wings like a spastic hummingbird. At last it landed on the table's edge and pranced across the *Times* to a plate of toasted bagel crumbs.

"Holy Mother of Christ," Jack said. "That bird almost gave me a heart attack."

"Lilly, it's OK," his wife said. "Pistachio didn't know his wings were clipped."

Lilly petted the bird's tiger-striped neck and confided "Pistachio can't speak any words, but he understands everything we say."

"Food," Jack said. "He understands food."

"Would you like to hold him?" the girl asked.

The penny-weight bird in my palm hopped on the rim of my coffee mug, pecked two sips, as if washing down crumbs, then marched up my sleeve with ticklish steps. It didn't stop until my collar, hiding out of my sight. I remained calm toward my shoulder guest, until it plucked a whisker, stinging my cheek with its question: What does it mean to be a man?

Creation

On the bench in white stretch pants I told
the quarterback I quit, but didn't admit
I couldn't stand up because my penis had snapped.
Both halves snug in my nylon crotch, bigger,
for sure, solid as dynamite, but what if
one should slip down my leg during a play?
"Finish the scenario," said my therapist.
"You're the writer. What would Hollywood do?"
Awake, I had a tough time completing dreams,
but after some silence I suggested reaching down
and throwing out my cold broken pipe.
"Marvelous," he said. "For next week
make yourself a new penis."

Something with feathers, I decided, something
with teeth. Not the penises of art history,
the wooden lap rockets on primitive carvings
or the floral codpieces on patriotic statues,
my organ would be furtive and wild,
a bark-eater, a nocturnal predator,
a burrower and a hibernator,
an omnivore grazing twenty hours a day,
eating its own weight in blackberries.

In time villagers would share theories—
Sasquatch, Wendigo—then a cryptic photo
of a golden eye on an abandoned road.
They'd argue over footprints, collect scat
not found in any field guide. They'd fear
what could come down from above the cliffs,
where the hunter fell, found three days later
with a ham sandwich still wrapped in his pocket.

I wasn't afraid of that mountain. All morning
I climbed animal trails past beech trees clawed
by bears, hemlocks shading owls and porcupines.
At the cliffs I filled my cup with water percolating
from moss, then scrambled up loose gully rocks.

Behind me, the valley haze twitched with dragon flies
and airborne seeds. A hawk screamed down the ridge.
I could sense it now: my penis smelled me approaching.
In the clearing where hobblebushes blossomed
with white saucers serving the fragrance of earth,
we would join in the dance that ignited the sun.

Trespassing at the Leap
--Platte Clove, Catskills

The sign said, "Strictly Forbidden."
I stepped over the guardrail and surged with happiness.
I dug my heels down the deer path of slippery duff
and grabbed the green paws of hemlock branches.
At the leap overlooking the gorge and waterfall,
I crawled to the edge and counted seconds,
as my spit dropped into rocks and ferns
of scree below. My groin tingled
with vertigo. After crawling back,
I rubbed off pebbles pressed in my palms.

How often had I seen this chasm painted?
The famous Devil's Kitchen and Bridal Veil Falls.
Yet as I sat where artists sit,
this scene refused to hold itself still,
not the forest leaves shimmying like sequins,
nor the valley humidity stirring with airborne seeds,
nor the slender waterfall shredding itself
into frothy diamonds. As a poet,
I wanted to join this flow.

I studied the vultures rocking on wings,
trolling the clove, then raised my arms in a V.
Impatient in the breeze, I leaped
and almost snagged my foot on a pitch pine
knotted to the cliff, then nearly shed my face
on a jutting bluestone brow spotted with lichen.
But somehow I soared into thickening air.
Pennies tumbled from my pocket like copper moths;
my falling wallet flapped like a bat.
Steadying my arms, I coasted into a thermal
that carried me high on a warm carousel.
Hunger awakened me to all the odors in the air.
I knew the smell of death I once feared
was what would sustain me now.

Utopian Poetry

How pathetic: the Sustainability Center forever unfinished.
A tar paper exterior. Insulation recycled from newsprint
leaking like feathers. Even the solar panels mere decorations.

Yet I didn't mind this utopian project attached to my cottage.
We shared a bathtub I sponged after the workman rinsed out
his brushes. Suddenly single again, I'd stink for three days,

while wrestling a poem to its finish: "Bubblegum Penises
at the Whitney Museum," for instance, my rant against irony.
Then I'd bathe for an hour, shampooing a spiky punk lather,

pinching my nose, submerging and counting to build up
my lungs as I had as a boy, when battleships ruled in my tub.
One morning the workman came early. Amber, his collie,

trotted into my cottage to sniff the compost bucket,
then shoved into the bathroom to drink from the toilet.
Always too eager, she licked at my lips, soap bubbles and all.

"Hey, it's a poet writing in a bathtub," said the workman,
delighted an old cliché could be true. A disciple of Sri Chinmoy,
he had a marathoner's lean body but wore knee braces

to stand all day on his ladder, plastering nail heads
smooth on the ceiling. The book of Sri Chinmoy poems
he lent me was marathon verse, poems #9,184 to #10,242

written one month in the Florida Keys, spiritual bromides
about palm trees and breathing. But the workman had kept it
in his glove compartment to study over lunch

after Amber tired of Frisbee. Now he asked how I liked it.
"Profound," I agreed from my bubbles, not having the heart
to admit the cover now had a shot glass stain
from a night I couldn't begin to explain.

Bosnia, Catskills

Remember the week military helicopters played hide-and-seek
in our mountains, hopping ridges and raking the forest
with propeller gusts? How fast they vanished?
Training for Bosnia, we read afterward in the papers.

So little did I know about that strife during my first years alone
in my cabin with no radio or health insurance,
my doorway guarded by nothing more than a phoebe's nest,
I decided to hike up for my own war rehearsal.

You ask, Why carry somebody else's misery
along with your day pack of fruit bars and compass,
spare socks and weathered copy of *Turtle Island*?
Isn't your own sadness good enough?

Yes, but please understand how little is needed
to imagine a pileated woodpecker hole as a stray explosion
the size of my face. What about the scattered bones,
the hobblebushes' heart-shaped leaves already turning

the bandage blood of autumn? My cherished solitude
grows sick with silence, as if a sniper is waiting for his shot.
This moment could be my last, kneeling
for nothing more than to check the freshness

of porcupine scat piled before a wedge in the rocks.
Or this: wondering if Bosnians heard the same song
after the helicopters left, the red-eyed vireo in the canopy:
Here-I-am. Where-are-you? Here-I-am. Where-are-you? Here-I-am.

You say, Perhaps you have a weakness for death.
We've seen you in our headlights, The one who stops
and wears work gloves to drag dead fawns off the road.
Haven't you learned how many are still to come?

Hungry, I choose a mossy log and unwrap a fruit bar,
while a chipmunk hunches at the end, fiercely shivering its tail.
I would answer these questions, but the contrail
climbing the blue sky has lost the innocence of clouds.

America

I've read your in-flight magazines.
I've known some of your people, a few hundred,
maybe more. But on the summit of Mt. Ajo, I ate lunch alone.

America, you should have seen me play in the desert below:
stick-batting sausage-like links off teddybear *cholla*,
then reattaching them by their own cactus velcro;
or plucking yellow bell pepper-like fruits
from barrel cacti to sample javelinas' cuisine;
or casting *saguaro* for cowboy cartoons,
one tall cactus throwing two short uppercuts,
another galloping bowlegged without leaving its trunk.

On the summit of Mt. Ajo I looked over three lands:
Arizona, Sonora, the Tohono O'Odham Indian Reservation.
The Indians ran a barbed wire fence up ridges
and rock spires, their border against cattle and Whites.
The Whites left a summit box rusted and padlocked.
The lone cedar defended itself, weathered branches
raised like antlers from its sprawling evergreen shrub.
Three nations naked with desert.
One car pulling a mile of dust on the park road below.

America, do you know how good pump water tastes
from a canteen? A tin of smoked oysters? Saltines?
America, whoever invented gorp deserves the Medal of Honor,
especially for this mix of dried bananas, coconut flakes,
cashews, and miniature carob kisses.
I brushed crumbs off my hands for the lizard.

America, your vast sky was so quiet
moments before the metallic scouring
I'd heard twice that morning but now finally saw:
three fighter jets tightening circles,
flashing razors of sunlight, suddenly aiming
to collide, then missing by eye-blinks.

America, I won't deny it: I was thrilled by your dogfight.
The jets circled again, this time for the kill;
two flaming streamers shed by the target plane
flamed out into curlicue skywriting,
skywriting I couldn't translate into words,
but it held for a minute as the sky's only cloud.
Far from its signal flares, the target jet rejoined the two
and flew in arrowhead formation over the reservation.

That's all I saw until opening night a month later in Baghdad.
And this story could end with unsettled feelings about empire,
but in America the story never really ends, now does it?

Off-trail I made a new route down from the saddle,
pausing to shake a flurry of seeds
from dried rattles on a century plant stalk,
then finding a cattle skull up to its eye sockets in sand.
I shook the skull clean, laid it teeth down
on a pedestal rock overlooking the desert plain
veined green by cactus-thick arroyos.

Down the loose slope my boots carved long slides,
as if skiing on sand. Then funneled
into a dry wash with pillow-smooth boulders,
I descended wary of rattlesnakes but surprised none.
Hopping and jumping down this natural jungle gym
for a thousand feet, I trusted sand traps
to be kind to my knees. How daring I grew,
sliding off boulders taller than myself, gamboling
like an overgrown boy. America,
I tell you, I was happy again.
What could beat this day in your mountains?
At bottom a *saguaro* waved a big hello.
A yellow-eyed thrasher sang w*hit-wheet!*
from the crown of its cactus.

In the arroyo I took a fresh compass bearing.
Only two miles round a ridge buttress to my tent.

Yet topping a rise I spotted trash strewn amid cactus:
golden potato chip foil pinned on a prickly pear,
two plastic water jugs punctured by needles,
an orange soda can rolled next to a rodent hole,
white cardboard from a cookie packet
tucked in the crotch of a *cholla*.
Who did this? Some high school doper or drunk?
Then I read labels: "Aqua Purificada,"
"Fanta Naranga," "Cremes de Vainilla."
The diet of illegals crossing forty miles at night
to avoid Border Patrol Jeep Cherokees.

America, you follow me everywhere.

America, My Friend

America, cancel your weather channel.
Come down to my dock to admire the bull frog,
shining his plump yellow chin on water under his chest.
His bubble eyes see everything and nothing.
Only the sight of a water snake would make this king jump.

America, forget about the score.
Watch the painted turtle flash red shoulders,
as her hind paws paddle loose sand to plant eggs.
We won't walk on that spot for the rest of the summer.
There's love everywhere, my friend:

Dragonflies mate on the wing.
Water lilies float like wedding carnations.
A breeze stampedes sparkling ruffles of sunlight
two hundred feet across the pond, then dies.
Its kin mourn in the pines. But a breeze needs nothing

to come back to life. Wait a minute, America,
you'll see it again. Did I tell you?
Last evening two beavers steered with black noses,
as if pacing twenty feet out from the dock.
Did we have an agreement? I knew they wanted

to come ashore to harvest more alders.
They knew I went in for nine o'clock jazz.
But this time I waited until stars floated so fat
on black water you could scoop one in your hands
to sip communion with sky.

The Troubadour Visits Loon Lake

I. Dusk

For twenty minutes Mik's eyes wouldn't budge
from the canoe paddle hung for ornament
above the deck's doors. No matter what I said
about Ted Hughes' two late wives or Hart Crane's leap,
Mik wanted to see the third bat I'd promised.
After sunset the first popped out from the paddle blade
turned bat house for the summer,
then puppet-flapped over Mik's curly hair.
Moments later the second wagged past his ear.
Now his glasses magnified white expectant eyes.

Until then we'd been having such a good discussion
about poets' suicides: Vachel Lindsay's Lysol,
Sara Teasdale's sleeping pills in her Village bathtub.
Fearless Mik, amused by poets' gothic lives,
Mik, who might explain the secret to enjoying what I wrote,
Mik, totally distracted in his Adirondack chair . . .

God damn it! I tilted up the paddle blade
to investigate my broken promise.
The third bat clung to scratchy panels:
a winged mouse, a furry turd, a corpse I feared.
"Nah," said Mik. "The old bugger's in for the night.
He got spooked, hearing about poets
who never played the flute." Mystery solved,
Mik serenaded owls hooting in the pines.

II. Dawn

Before first coffee I led Mik with his flute
to the pond. Sunrise herded rising mist
like ghost seahorses toward shoreline pines.
At the dock I unlatched the gate of dewy thread
by its piling guy lines, a spider web
rigged each night to snag a moth or two.
The spider charged down its pole to hide
beneath the planks, sure to weave again tonight.

"Yesterday I saw a web on the ferry prow," said Mik,
who'd crossed Lake Champlain from Vermont.
"It flapped but never broke. It held up in a hurricane,
if you're spider-size. But I've seen webs
where you'd never think to look: toll booths,
urinals, jail cells when I've performed in prisons.
Anyone who steps on spiders doesn't understand
the ancient myth they wove the alphabet,
then left poets to do the best we can with words."
On his flute Mik played a spider's song, or so he said.

Sister Scarecrows

-- Cottekill Fire House Community Garden

Drunk? Or simply exhausted? The scarecrow slumps
in a castoff chair. Her faceless nylon stocking
stuffed with newspapers for a head
flops backwards to stare at the flawless sky
that hasn't rained since July. Her work gloves
magic-marked "BOSS" across the knuckles
lay empty on her lap. With one ankle
skinny as a broomstick and the other
no ankle at all, she sits like a starveling
before her crop of stunted vines.

But her sister, dressed in similar green sweats
that forgive her sagging breasts and spreading hips,
sits upright and alert, her straw hat tipped
outrageously sideways with bohemian flare.
Her name tag says "Sunshine." Her work gloves
cradle a dirt-cheeked doll with blue eyes and golden hair.
She's slipped off her leather pumps
and snuggled her broomsticks in raspberry brambles
now ripening with fruit despite the drought.
Watering my peppers, I swear she asks for a cigarette.

Then she whispers that her bitter sister
has become a desert mystic convinced
the seed she planted will be the burning bush.
She, herself, would settle for a good mint julep
and a man who still believes in wearing teeth.

Pride of Pumpkins

Of one hundred pumpkin faces
candle-lit on farm-stand bleachers,
how many do you recognize from town?
The mayor: does he have tic-tac-toe for a face?
Or a sports car for a smile? The romance columnist,
who advises country women meeting new mechanics
every week, has eyebrows carved like scythes.
The banker could only be the $ sign,
the plumber has a crescent wrench for a nose.
The homeless woman who plays saint on the green,
blessing traffic in her year-round hooded coat;
she must be the question mark, flickering,
as if it might go out. Which are you, my love,
glowing on the shelves? Heart-shaped lips
plumped up for a kiss? Almond eyes open to
an orange soul? Do you wear diamonds?
Or is the marijuana leaf your sign?
Do you have bat-wing ears or lopsided eyes,
as if you must be from that other planet,
a place I know all too well myself?
If only you'd wink among one hundred
pumpkins, I'd be happy then to be faceless,
but full of pulp and full of seed.

Pagans

After the March rains I masturbate
over the thawed soil to plant more of us.
Hatched naked as mushrooms, we never grow
the green skin needed to survive by the sun alone,
so we must step off our roots, hungry
and curious, perfectly disguised
as fellow humans, cocky and protected
by ethical principles, scientific understanding.
Then a bee crawls in our ear to pollinate
the thousand folds of our brain.

Laden with the dewy residue
of dreams and Godly visions, the bee
grows too heavy to fly but can't stop buzzing
anymore than we can explain this sudden desire
to roll naked in mud, cloak ourselves
in seeds and minerals, dress in trumpet vines
that blossom and feed hummingbirds
at our breasts. Earth again, we forget the reason
we could be anything but pagans.

Trickster

I tried to persuade a porcupine to uncloak its quills,
become pettable, enjoy the human touch.
Who knows what came over me?
Perhaps Fox News.

What Kind of Mind Invented the Golf Ball?
--Devil's Notch, Catskills

Like this one buried up to its dimpled white crown
in damp silt between maple roots, so cocky
and clean, so perfect. All morning I've picked up trash
in this notch, where ravens broadcast from cliffs
and shadbushes hold smoke blossoms into May.
I've filled my yellow bag with the transparent brain
of a baggie submerged in a stream, Bud cans so faded
their words appear Russian, a paint can that burped
its last gob of white latex onto a stone wall—
the burial mound for bottle glass, burger clamshells,
a condom. The dead porcupine I boot-toed off the road
left a toothpick trail of quills. But a golf ball?
It doesn't belong here! Not this alien probe
from manicured suburbs, where I served my youth
pushing mowers and painting garages. Only once
did I place my faith in my hands gripping
a golf club. At 17 I swung with fury and power,
topping weak grounders down the fairway,
or lofting grass divots I didn't bother to replace.

What kind of mind invented the golf ball?
The same that invented the cover girl's pout?
The perfect, unattainable sonnet? The insult
so clever and true it lives under your skin for life?

I lift the golf ball from its silt pocket,
dimpled eyes no different than dimpled chin.
I bounce it hard on the pavement, a bounce
it obviously loves, hopping over my head.
Even on Mars it would feel at home,
never lonely, hungry, or broke.
How can you make a golf ball cry?
How can you make it understand?

A Natural History of Cigarette Butts
--Devil's Notch, Catskills

Deep in prickly briar wands unclawing leaves
for May lies an open pack of Parliaments,
revealing nibbled foil, cigarettes tightly packed
yet trimmed of every filter. Did a mouse
harvest cotton for its nest? If so, may we
call this hope? My mother smoked,

smoked and had a throat scar like a nipple.
As a child to shame her into quitting, I ate
her Parliaments in front of guests and choked
on filters. I coughed with terrifying dryness,
until a man bent me on his knees and pounded
on my back. She thought I was dying.

One by one I pick them from roadside gravel
or straw-like gully grass woven down by runoff:
cotton filters wrapped white or caramel.
All morning I've collected trash in this notch,
where larger garbage should fill my yellow bag.
My mother quit, but I can't seem to stop.

My Mother's Last Summer

Propped up on pillows,
    she whispers her fear:
        Something's burning.

I reassure her
    the nursing home's
        built out of cinder blocks,

her curtains,
    flame-retardant plastic.
        If she smells anything burning,

it's probably toast.
    I'm lying.
        All I can smell

are sunflowers burning,
    the drought
        she once fought

every morning
    with sprinkler
        and hose.

The Bargain

Was your nose always crooked, pinched,
and pressed over lopsided nostrils? Or was it punched
by the stroke that inflated your feet and stiffened
your fingers like chopsticks, struggling to hold
your afternoon tea, a plastic cup of tepid Lipton's
from the nursing home commissary?

I didn't know caskets came in cardboard printed
with wood grain I remember from cheap apartments.
You look so small under this white blanket, Mom.
Your forehead's cold as a cobblestone,
but I know you've been in refrigeration for two days.
Can I laugh now? Is it true your fingernails keep growing?

Your nails never looked right without gardening dirt,
did they? Too clean and medical. Remember your nurse
who painted them red for Valentine's Day,
thinking you were the kind of woman who admired
Elizabeth Taylor? You mistook your red nails
for your period. For ten years, you thought I was 23
and married to my cousin Muggsie.
You smelled something burning every time
you meant to say you were hungry.

Mom, you look better without glasses. On visits
my gift was to wash off the smudges and dandruff,
not that your magnified eyes could follow the Trinitron
your nurses turned to tennis matches or holiday parades.
One autumn I brought a shopping bag of vermilion leaves,
but you asked if we had enough toilet paper at home.

Dad's at the front desk bargaining for the plain headstone,
$200 off catalog. It doesn't matter to me, Mom,
but you wouldn't like these plastic flowers, either.

Can I tell you a secret? We've already picked up the Trinitron
at the nursing home, said good-bye and good riddance
to your roommate who was wailing like a widow
— "Marcus Milk, Marcus Milk"—from reading her lunch.

Dad folded your lighthouse quilt and Christmas dresses.
I waited until he left, then sat in your wheelchair
with its hard rubber cushion and lifted my legs
into the foot stirrups. I pointed my toes for you, Mom,
like a ballerina. I made my own bargain
with the bastards of fate.

Drinking Sherry With My Mother

The month before college, I read *The History of the SDS*
and *The Electric Kool-Aid Acid Test* to prepare for freshman year
in California. Since June, I'd saved $2,000, caulking boats
and painting garages. So I took off September, swimming
two miles at the beach if the jellyfish weren't bad,
then flirting with the blonde life guard in a tennis visor,
who still had a year at Greenwich High.

Yet I always rode home for five o'clock sherry,
or a fruity white wine with a floating strawberry,
or whatever my mother had in mind for afternoon tea.
At the patio table we acted casually, me with my towel
still knotted round my neck like a cape from my bicycle ride,
my mother still in her old tennis dress from weeding.
To be honest, we'd never had drinks before.
Maybe she wanted to teach me how before college,
fearing I'd turn to harder drugs like my cousin.
Or perhaps she was lonely for serious conversation.
That month I was brilliant on the importance
of voting for Carter, the dawning future of solar power,
the American novel after Pynchon and McGuane.

The funny thing was she didn't disagree,
didn't pester me about my unmade bed or unkept promise
to prune hedges. She poured me a second glass
and smiled with a faint sadness I didn't understand.
Not until the kitchen timer rang, reminding her
to marinate the salmon teriyake, did she snap back:
Would I please light the citronella candle
on the patio table, so we could have dinner outdoors
without getting bitten? The wick burned so slowly,
I smelled citronella long after she'd gone to bed.
Alone on the patio, I dreamed of California
as the land where girls wore shorts until December
and hippies farmed naked in communes.

Living with Sanka on the Lazy Susan

Dad didn't understand the coffee maker, either,
so he poured us hot water for Sanka,
cleared a month of *Business Week* and *Fortune*
from the kitchen table draped in the waxy green cloth
meant for the patio in my mother's day.
Waterproof, slug-proof, flame-retardant,
this poncho-slick cloth would have stayed out in snow
before she allowed it as linen, but my father didn't know.
Living alone during her decade in the nursing home,
he'd fumbled through chores. The refrigerator shelf still held
her plastic polar bear of baking soda now long expired
as deodorizer. The sink sponge had crumbled,
the carving knife had snapped its point, the digital clock
had blinked 3:17 for years. Now he wondered
if I'd like Swanson's French toast popped in the toaster.

Yesterday at the funeral he'd smiled at my eulogy
to her recipes: oyster stew on his birthday,
Thanksgiving pumpkin baked with apples and rice,
the Wickendon family plum pudding soused with brandy
and flambéed after Christmas dinner.
My favorite was the refrigerator pitcher of ice tea
with its jungle of mint clippings and sunken lemon halves.
All summer she thickened the mix, adding rose hips
and orange peels, cloves and sassafras roots,
an aquarium deep-sea diver for a joke.
Like sourdough starter her refrigerator tea
only grew better with age. Not until November
did we dump the pitcher's soggy heap in the compost.

I had no appetite for his offering of frozen French toast.
Instead, I'd take my father to his first Starbucks
for cappuccinos and pastries nearly as tasty
as the hot cross buns she baked Sunday mornings.
The poor man was starving. And so was I.

My Late Mother as a Ruffed Grouse

-- Ashokan High Point, Catskills

Never before had a grouse failed to explode
from the underbrush with a wing-beating panic,
a feathered cannonball fanning a leaf-ripping tail.
But this bird didn't budge. It kept pecking
at leaf litter as methodically as a maid
checking under cushions for coins.
For several minutes, I focused my binoculars
on its ladybug eyes, its black-banded tail,
but didn't want to spoil the magic by staying too long.

Bushwhacking through acres of mountain laurel,
I navigated tangled stalks like woody barbed wire.
Finally, a boulder ramp led me down to a clearing.
But which direction to the reservoir lookout,
rumored to lie east of the blueberry bald,
I couldn't sense any better than from above.
Behind me, I spotted the grouse half-sliding,
half-hopping on clownish chicken feet to catch up.
It stopped on the rock, cocked its head sideways,
then eyeballed me with an orange intensity.
Oh yes, I remembered that look,
unblinking, undeterred, unashamed
of being in charge, yet being in love.

Could this bird really be my late mother?
At her burial last winter I scattered grouse feathers
to honor her passion as an Audubon birder.
Did I unwittingly plant the seed for her return?
Crippled by strokes, she lived so long in a nursing home
she had no idea I lived in a cabin, not Hoboken
or Manhattan. To her, I was always 23 and married,
for some unfathomable reason, to my cousin Muggsie.

This grouse clearly knew what she wanted.
Softly she cooed and finally winked.
I murmured my best grouse impersonation,
eager to talk no matter what we happened to say.

I sat on the grass, an invitation she accepted
to prance close to my boots, cocky as a city pigeon.
For her country outing, she'd dressed
in subdued browns and whites, but make no mistake:
her feathered crest sharpened her head.
When her blinking turned almost flirtatious,
I lowered my eyes, apparently a fresh invitation,
for she paraded alongside my leg, pausing
every few steps to nip at a blueberry flower.
With my hands I could have cradled her like a dove,
cooing, content. Was that what she wanted?
Behind my back, she pecked at my daypack zipper.

How could I explain my bachelor's cabin,
the dirty socks from last week's hike still hanging
on the upstairs railing, the dirty dishes forever
crowding the sink? Did she think
she'd be satisfied eating seeds from a bowl
made of plastic and sharing my cold wooden floor
with the mice? Didn't she know
I could be arrested for bringing a grouse home
under the Wildlife Protection Act?
Did she know how rarely I swept?

No, I needed to end this strange encounter.
I stood and shouldered my pack, nodded good-bye.
But giant steps up the rock didn't do any good.
She hopped up her own crooked ladder
of laurel stalks, then paused at the next dirt patch
for me to catch up. How could I shake her?
Whenever I plunged in a new direction,
climbing and tripping through bushes,
she scampered nearby, easily low-hurdling
trunk tangles and roots. I barged like an oaf,
but she didn't act disappointed in me as a grouse.
She waited and cooed with encouragement.
Not until I broke loose on the blueberry bald
did she stop at the edge of her laurel protectorate.

Yet no matter how long I rested on the only boulder,
pretending to admire the quixotic flight
of black butterflies sampling blueberry nectar,
I knew she waited with unbending love and devotion
in the bushes I couldn't avoid to hike home.

Will Nixon grew up in the Connecticut suburbs, lived in Hoboken and Manhattan, then moved to a Catskills log cabin, and now lives in Woodstock, New York. As a journalist, he was a contributing editor to *The Amicus Journal*, published by the Natural Resources Defense Council, and a correspondent for the *Adirondack Explorer*. His poetry chapbooks are *When I Had It Made* (Pudding House) and *The Fish Are Laughing* (Pavement Saw). His poems have appeared in such journals as *The Ledge, Rattle, Slipstream, Wisconsin Review,* and many others. His work has been nominated for a Pushcart Prize and and listed in *The Best American Essays of 2004*.

$16.00   FootHills Publishing   ISBN: 978-0-941053-72-3